How to Succe̶ ̶ ̶
Your BC Property Assessment

A How- to Guide for
British Columbia Homeowners

By: Peter D. Morris
With: Tim Down

© 2014 Peter D. Morris

ISBN 978-0-9938774-2-1

Published By:

Greenstead Media
Mill Bay, BC, Canada

Important Disclaimer

This guide is designed to provide information that may assist a homeowner to appeal their own property assessment within the province of British Columbia. It is sold with the understanding that the publisher and authors are not engaged in rendering legal, accounting or other professional advice or services. If legal or other expert advice is required, the services of competent professionals should be engaged.

The authors and publisher shall have no liability or responsibility to any entity or person with respect to any loss or damage caused directly or indirectly or alleged to have been caused directly or indirectly by the information contained in this guide.

Due to the nature of the assessment appeal process neither the authors nor the publisher warrant or guarantee that anyone will obtain a reduction in their property assessment; and in fact, there is always the risk that the assessed value could be increased upon appeal.

CONTENTS

Introduction

The elderly gentleman stood in front of the Property Assessment Review Panel arguing that the Panel had no right to tell him what his taxes should be. He argued the panel didn't live in his neighborhood and the city didn't keep the street as clean as other areas of town so why should he pay more taxes?

I'm Peter D. Morris. I knew at that time I needed to write this short, but highly informative book. This gentleman wanted to find a way to lower his property taxes but was at a complete loss how to do it. Needless to say the panel didn't adjust his assessment.

In these pages you will learn:
- Why you should appeal your assessment,
- How to determine if you should appeal your assessment
        (*in some cases you shouldn't*),
- How your assessment was made by the assessor,
- How to find the right information you need to support your case,
- Who and when you should discuss your assessment with and
- How to successfully present your position.

I have successfully appealed the property tax assessments on my houses for years saving hundreds of dollars each time. I use many of the same techniques and principles as I use in my role as a 30+ year veteran commercial property asset manager appealing the assessments on office buildings, shopping centres and industrial buildings. I will share these insights with you.

You may be thinking a house isn't the same as an office building. As you read this book you will learn that many of the principles of commercial property assessment apply and can be used in your appeal. You will use these in a simplified version, so it is not difficult or complicated to appeal your own property tax assessment.

However, you would be right that appealing the tax assessment on an office building or shopping centre is a far more complicated task. When I needed to do that I turned to an expert in property tax assessments. I called Tim Down AACI, P. App, CAE, RI(BC), CLHMS. And once again, when writing this for your success I've called upon Tim to be my co-author.

Tim Down has been actively involved in the real estate valuation, consulting and sales for over 20 years throughout British Columbia. Tim's career started out as a fee appraiser based in Vancouver and he worked throughout the Lower Mainland. He was an Appraisal Supervisor with the BC Assessment Authority for 11 years. He joined Colliers International in Vancouver as Director of Property Tax Services for Western Canada in 2001. He was also Vice-President of Property Tax Services with PricewaterhouseCoopers LLP in Vancouver.

Tim is a professionally accredited real estate practitioner holding the following designations and licenses:

- AACI, P. App (Appraisal Institute of Canada)
- CAE (International Association Of Assessing Officers)
- RI(BC) (Real Estate Institute of British Columbia)
- Licensed Sales Representative (Okanagan Mainline Real Estate Board)
- Member of the Canadian Property Tax Institute

Tim currently provides property tax and real estate consulting services through his company, PacWest Commercial Real Estate Advisors, centrally based in Kelowna, BC. Tim is also an active real estate sales professional specializing in executive, estate and waterfront home sales as well as investment, commercial and industrial property sales throughout the Okanagan Corridor. He is the founding Chair of OMREB's Commercial Zone and Past Chair of the BC Commercial Council.

So let's get started by first looking at how your property tax bill is created.

How your Property Tax is Created

Many people will say they are appealing their property taxes. In reality, they aren't. It is just a simple way of conveying the whole thought of reducing their property or real estate taxes. In this chapter we will go over the process that is used to create the annual property tax notice you receive around mid-May each year.

The gentleman at the Property Assessment Review Panel hearing you met in the introduction didn't really understand this and that was his first mistake.

The appeal process is in three steps as follows:

Your property tax bill reflects the BC Assessment Authority's opinion of value, classification and exemptions for assessment purposes which is then used as the basis to apply property tax rates reflecting the various taxing agencies and jurisdictions in the subject property's area. For simplicity, we will refer to municipal taxes, school taxes, water taxes and other taxes on your bill as the same since the following outline generally applies. We should also note that although we will look at each as individual steps with one following the other, they generally occur simultaneously.

Step One

The county, municipality or regional district where you live and who you pay taxes to, are required to develop an operating budget covering all the aspects of services where you live, including police, fire, garbage collection, road maintenance, parks and recreation, city hall, etc.

If you are really concerned about how your local government is managing your property tax dollars and are civically minded then we encourage you attend city council or regional district meetings, talk to the city manager or even consider running for office. However, all of this is beyond the scope of this book.

Once all the annual operating costs have been tallied for your town, city or county, they then have a provisional budget to estimate the total rate of taxation for all classes of assessed property.

Step Two

The British Columbia Assessment Authority (BCAA) is required by law to provide these taxation authorities (municipalities, regional districts, etc) with an annual valuation of all the properties in British Columbia. This valuation document is called the Annual Assessment Roll, which identifies the legal description, civic address, property classification, property assessment value of land and improvements as well as any exemptions for all properties. The valuation date is July 1 of the previous year but the assessor also has to consider the physical condition and actual use of the property as at October 31 of the previous year as well.

The BCAA produces an annual taxable property assessment roll that reflects the entire assessment values (less exemptions) of all properties based on their classification for the taxation authorities review and consideration. There are currently 9 classes of property with the residential and business classes comprising the majority of all properties on the assessment roll in terms of overall numbers as well as values. The BCAA then adds up all the residential and business values in your community or assessment area and gives this number to the tax authority. Since the total assessed value of all the property in your area is so large, they divide the number by 1000.

Step Three

The annual operating budget created by the municipality (taxing jurisdiction) is divided by the total assessed value, as determined by the BCAA for that taxing jurisdiction. In British Columbia, the local taxing authorities set their own property tax rates for each of the 9 classes of property. The actual formula in the creation of these tax rates is a lot more complicated than we've outlined here but this is intended to give you an overview of the mechanics of the property taxation system in BC. The revenue required from the annual operating budget is then split into the burden that each class of property will carry as a percentage of the whole.

Each class of property has its property tax rate determined by dividing the total assessed value for the entire class of property by the total property tax burden expected from that class of property. **This is called the mill rate or rate of taxation.** The "Residential" Mill Rate is then multiplied by the assessed value of your house to arrive at the property tax you owe on your property tax bill.

There are three fundamental variables in this method, for those mathematically inclined.

The first is the budget created by your municipality. And unless you go to those dreadfully long and mostly boring meetings you really have to trust that your elected officials and those hired to look after such things are working on your behalf.

The second is the value of all of the property in your class and in your taxation area. This makes up the denominator creating part of the mill rate. Here, you don't have any say on this number but you wish it to be REALLY big, while the budget is really small.

The third is the value of your property. This really is the only area you can influence greatly. This is the area we focus on in this book.

As we continue you will see why you can actually reduce your property taxes, not only against what would have occurred if you didn't appeal your assessment but year over year.

Why You Should Appeal Your Property Assessment

When we tell friends and neighbors we are appealing our property assessment some will ask why. A few believe that a lower assessed value means that the house is worth less if they were to sell it.

That is an understandable concern but for 98% of people it really shouldn't be…. and here is why.

Yes, we have all seen real estate ads that say: "Priced below assessed value" and many residential sale websites list the assessed value on the same page as the asking price. The natural conclusion is that what you would sell your house for is closely tied to the assessed value. In truth, it generally isn't.

Remember that the BCAA produces an assessment value as at July 1 each year, but you get your notice many months later. In a rapidly rising market, the price you may sell your house for may be much more than its value even a week ago let alone many months ago. In a rapidly falling market, the opposite is true.

Most people still live in their houses for many years so the prospect of the assessed value affecting the actual sales price is never really a factor.

And if you did have to sell your property shortly after successfully getting a reduced assessment, a good real estate agent will tell the buyer all the benefits of the lower tax bill.

Other friends and neighbors believe an ever-increasing assessed value is a good thing and validates their purchase. That too seems reasonable....but remember the second variable from the last chapter?

What you wish for is a very big *overall* assessed value for your class of property – not your *individual* assessed value. In a coming chapter, and as we work to present the best case for lowering your assessment, we will show you how your assessment may be higher than your neighbors and increasing faster than your neighbors. This artificially increases your share of the overall tax bill. We don't mind paying for our fair share of the services we receive but we shouldn't have to pay part of neighbor Bill's share too.

Some friends and relatives believe that if we reduce our own property assessments then the city won't have enough money to run government, keep the schools open or police the streets. Hopefully, we've shown you that wouldn't be the case in British Columbia, since the government creates its annual operating budget that is then divided by the total annual assessed values in the entire property class. A change in the assessed values would cause the mill or tax rate to go up per $1000 of value but the municipality would always have enough money to operate based on its budget requirements.

The same can't be said if they can't keep to their budget but legislation in British Columbia requires local governments to operate with balanced budgets so that they do not runs deficits nor do they accrue budget surpluses. However, that is for another discussion. But then, everyone makes mistakes. And that is another reason to appeal your assessment. We will show you why mistakes happen in the assessment process and how you can use these as the basis for winning your appeal.

The final reason to appeal your assessment is that any reduction in assessed value will save money when you are successful and, some of us just find the challenge of appealing interesting and fun.

Why You Shouldn't Appeal Your Assessment.

Any property assessment that is appealed CAN be decreased, remain the same or can be increased. The filing of an appeal against a property assessment notice will automatically draw direct attention from the local assessor. The assessor will contact the appellant (usually the property owner but third parties can appeal any property, without fee, with Property Assessment Review Panel) review their valuation methodology and calculations to confirm their information and correct any errors that may have been made. This review by the assessor may lead to an assessment valuation to be increased if the Review Panel believes there is more evidence and support to the assessor's revised reasoning than your reasons for requesting a reduction. So here are a few reasons why you shouldn't appeal your property assessment:

1. When you are about to sell your property, particularly if the sale will happen just before the property tax bill is due. Why waste your time if you won't see a benefit?

2. When you have completed your investigations and can't find a discrepancy in the assessor's information, valuation of your property and the assessment values

15

of neighbourhood properties are similar. We will show you how to review the assessor's records, investigate neighbourhood comparable assessment values and verify the data. Once again, an appeal would be a waste of your time because there is little reason to adjust your assessed value.

3. When you can't uncover a compelling argument why your assessment is wrong. The Review Panel has no mandate to alter any property assessment value based on an appellant's perceived quality or lack of public services (paved streets, garbage collection, sidewalks, streetlights, etc) that their property taxes pay for.

4. If you appealed your property assessment at least once before in the previous two years and won. The assessor or the Review Panel may feel you have become an annoyance and time waster if the same issues of the previous appeal(s) have been corrected and reflected for the current property assessment year. While the Review Panel has an obligation to impartially hear every appeal based on each appeal's merit, commonsense usually prevails.

Appraisal 101

OK, so we have reviewed the appeal process Let's now delve into how the BC Assessment Authority assesses properties for property tax purposes. Understanding this will give you the knowledge you need to review and focus when undertaking your initial investigation.

First, a disclaimer. Appraisal is both a science and an art that takes many years and much learning and practice to understand and complete with acceptable accuracy. It is understood that you will not be an authority on appraisal or assessment valuation from reading these few words. If you require a professional valuation for any reason, we highly recommend you seek the services of an accredited real estate appraiser. That said, it is normal practice for owners of residential properties to prepare and represent their issues and concerns themselves before the Property Assessment Review Panel (at the Property Assessment Review Panel you will be called an Appellant). In order to be successful, appellants need to be familiar with the following traditional appraisal valuation methodologies used by the assessor::

    a.   The Income Approach

    b.   The Cost (or Replacement) Approach

    c.   The Direct Comparison Approach

The Income Approach

This valuation approach typically is not applicable for the valuation of single-family dwellings, townhouses and stratified residences. It is used to value income producing properties such as apartment buildings, office buildings, shopping centres and other investment, commercial and industrial properties. Even if you have a basement suite that you rent out, the assessor will not use this approach to value your home.

If you do have an income producing property we strongly recommend you to do two things: commit to a review of your annual property assessment and hire a professional property tax agent, such as Tim, to assist you.

The Cost Approach

This valuation approach is based on the theory that the value of a property can be broken down into two separate valuation components; land value plus depreciated value of the improvements to the land (buildings). The appraiser first determines the value of the site as though it is vacant and then adds the depreciated "replacement" value of the buildings to determine an overall value. The challenge with this approach remains that it is difficult to fully determine the impact of depreciation on the value of the improvements and is most useful when buildings are newer and current land sales are available. For this reason, this approach is generally used as a backup approach or in cases where there is limited sales activity. This type of appraisal is typically used for such things as calculating how much insurance you should have, art valuation, etc. It is also used when it is helpful to determine the future value of something.

The Direct Comparison Approach

This approach is based on the theory that the value of a property can be determined by reviewing the sale of "similar" or "comparable" properties that have recently sold in the property's neighbourhood. This is the approach that the BC Assessment Authority relies upon in their review, analysis and valuation of residential properties throughout the Province of British Columbia. This approach also requires significant "subjective" adjustments by an assessor when comparing sales evidence as no two properties are ever exactly alike. Most people do the same thing when they are looking to purchase or sell real estate or an automobile.

You will find one house advertised and may compare it to yours. Does it have as large a lot, view, waterfront, more or less bedrooms and bathrooms, is it larger or smaller, does it have basement, what other amenities does it have (garage, sundeck, pool, hot tub, etc.), what is the quality and condition of the interior finish, is it on a busy street, in a cul-de-sac or next to a golf course?

For a used car you would check for damage, mileage, interior wear, maintenance records, extra bells and whistles and if it was driven by the little ol' lady from Pasadena. You would then judge the asking price against the asking prices of other similar cars.

You probably do the same thing in the aisles of your supermarket without much thought, comparing one can of soup to another. And we'll bet you even did this comparison on the price of this book against the potential property tax savings. You may mentally do all this comparison in a few seconds in your head and then declare that the price seems reasonable or not.

The assessor does the same thing, but in a far more methodical and detailed manner because she or he has to justify their valuation to you, your neighbours, the local government as well as the Property Assessment Review Panels and Appeal Boards. The assessor can't simply declare a value without strong analytical support as to how they arrived at their annual property assessment values.

Did you just have an "Aha" moment?

> The best way to have your property value assessment lowered is to find and point out that the comparison wasn't really an apples to apples comparison and that there may have been errors in any subjective adjustments made by the assessor to account for any of the differences.

But we are not done yet explaining how a property is to be appraised.

There are also twelve principles that should guide the assessor. Two will be most beneficial to you and they are:

1. Was the property assessment at market value? In other words, was there market sales evidence of similar properties around the date of July 1 that supports the assessor's assessed value? Are the assessor's valuation assumptions and subjective adjustment supported by market evidence?

2. Is the assessed value "equitable" when compared to the assessments of similar and competing properties in the neighbourhood? Can it stand the test of being compared to a wide range of other assessments? Essentially, the assessor can't single out your

property if it was recently purchased or renovated without taking into consideration what is happening in the global neighbourhood.

These two principles are critical if any appeal will be successful so it is crucial that homeowners demonstrate that the assessor's assessment valuation and equity comparisons are not fair or equitable. We will show you how to use these principles of fair and equitable to your advantage. For example, one of the tenets of appraisal is this: the market price is "the most probable sale price of a property in terms of money in a competitive and open market, assuming that the buyer and seller are acting prudently and knowledgeably, allowing for a sufficient time for the sale, and assuming that the transaction is not affected by undue pressures."

We put this in quotations because we simply didn't make up that convoluted line. It is the industry-accepted definition that the assessor will use in determining the value of your real estate for property assessment purposes.

Here is an example of how one of us, used this to his advantage to significantly reduce his property assessment a number of years ago.

The assessor based the value of his property upon the recorded price paid for the property on June 1. Remember that the assessor uses the market price as of July 1 *[Just one month later].* The assessor's argument was that the price paid for the property occurred just before the assessor's valuation date so it must reflect the market price.

The assessor didn't know – and couldn't know unless it was brought it up on appeal –that one of us was being transferred from a higher priced housing market and had only 72 hours to locate and purchase a house for his family. The seller, who was a real estate agent, was aware of this this time constraint and the buyer overpaid for his house relative to the general market in the neighbourhood.

The argument at appeal was:

1. The price he paid was not market, but was above market and therefore didn't fit the definition of the most probable price in a competitive open market,
2. The buyer, was not prudent and knowledgeable given the short time frame and relocating from a completely different market, and
3. the 72 hour time frame he had to find and settle a sale created an undue pressure.

Here is the definition again, and this time we've underlined the points made to the appeal board.

"The most probable sale price of a property in terms of money in a competitive and open market, assuming that the buyer and seller are acting prudently and knowledgeably, allowing for a sufficient time for the sale, and assuming that the transaction is not affected by undue pressures."

He also had to show what he felt was a market price that fit the definition – just as we will show you.

In this real-life example, you see how the assessor thought the valuation was correct based on the recorded sale price and why you should always investigate your assessed values. If the buyer had not investigated his property's assessed value against others in the area – which reflected the actual price he paid for the house, and may have seemed reasonable on the surface, he would have remained assessed at an above market assessment and paid too much in property taxes in the following years.

Also, from this example, you can now see that it isn't just the physical characteristics of any property that need to be considered but also the nature of the actual sales of individual properties.

The conditions of any sale are extremely important when considering whether a property is comparable or not. If the parties are related, or special financing was obtained, or the seller was forced to sell by some condition of their life (a move, divorce, death, etc.) are all conditions that would have an influence on the price of any particular property, either up or down.

These are general comments about property appraisal. We hope that you now have a better understanding of how the assessor thinks and how they must act for property assessment purposes in determining the value of your house and everyone else's too.

How To Assess Hundreds Of Thousands Of Homes Every Year

The most accurate valuation would be a physical inspection of every home and a detailed comparison of that home with every other home in the same market all at the same point in time. That would be impossible. Therefore, the BC Assessment Authority applies what statisticians call "secondary data" to make a reasonable assumption of the fair market value.

Before you cry foul, consider that this is how most prices are set. When a real estate agent suggests a selling price or an offer price on a home, they are using general market data and their personal experience as a guide. The general data is a secondary source. If you were to look at a few cars to buy, you may look for prices in the newspaper or online. That too is secondary data. You don't actually inspect every car listed to determine if it's a fair market price.

The land title system in British Columbia is called a Torrens system, the land title system developed by Robert Torrens in Australia in the last century. Torrens opined that every piece of property should be listed on a registry and every transaction should be recorded. There are now over 1.9 Million registered titles in British Columbia.

The BC Assessment Authority has legislated access to all the land titles and property transactions registered. Using their proprietary computer system, attempts to edit, review and analyze all the sales in each market, to make comparisons and then attempts to spot check the results by personally inspecting any properties that appear to be outliers. The assessor starts with a basic analysis ratio or metric called the "Assessment to Sales Ratio" or ASR, which divides the current assessment value by the "actual" or "adjusted" sale price value. The BC Assessment Authority has traditionally set the ASR rate at 97% for residential properties in urban areas. If a property has a low or high indicated ASR level, the assessor is obligated to investigate the individual sale and property assessment data.

The assessor also relies on a second statistical analysis called the "Coefficient of Dispersion" or COD. This statistical measure evaluates the distribution or range of sold property assessment values. The assessor has historically set the COD for residential properties in urban areas at 10%.

These statistical measures are based on good standing property assessment practices but they still do not tell the whole story. The challenge always remains that the assessor has scarce resources to be applied to the greatest return. This means that the BC Assessment Authority must determine on an annual basis, which property types and classes should be inspected. International standards state that wholesale reassessment (inspections of property) should be completed every 6 years and no later than every 10 years. The reality is that the assessor rarely undertakes a true physical reassessment; but instead opts for inspection by telephone, by MLS data review, by surveys or self-reporting mail out questionnaires, and contacting real estate agents and appraisers.

This method also does something else, which you never see on your property assessment notice.

It produces **a range of values** for a 'typical' property. By default then, it will produce a range of assessment values for all properties. The assessment value applied to your property may not be the lowest value in the range of similar and competing properties in your neighbourhood.

The reason for this is that the BC Assessment Authority uses statistical software that has to look at thousands of sales and it is unlikely that any two properties are identical. So this software must be manipulated or adjusted by the assessor to reflect any differences in value for a variety reasons (location, size, condition, quality, design, age, etc). Just as in polls you read or hear on the radio there is always a margin for error. Although that margin is generally considered acceptable, it is in your interests to get your specific property assessment to the lowest end of the property assessment value range.

We trust this is all starting to make sense and you can begin to see where there is room to challenge the value placed on your property. However, we must stop here and point out that the assessor isn't false, incompetent or even working against you. The truth of the matter is that it is impossible and impractical to conduct an individual review of every property every year. As a result, systems are employed to get 'close enough' and fair to everyone.

It is the individual property owner's responsibility to double check the information and work *with* the assessor to create a value for their own property.

Your Property Tax Assessment Notice and the Steps to Appeal

Before we go onto the next steps let's review what you now know:

-   You know how your property taxes are created
-   You know why you should appeal your property value assessment (and when you shouldn't)
-   You know a little about the valuation methodology and
-   You know how that all gets done every year.

We've also shed light on some of the avenues you can explore to appeal your assessment.

Before we show you some of the ways to structure your argument let's review the actual process you will follow to appeal your assessment.

It all starts with your notice from the Assessment Authority. Actually, we will show you in a later chapter why you really want to start the process BEFORE the notice, but for now we'll start at the notice.

These are typically sent out at the end of each year and received while you are still regretting the New Year resolutions.

If you wish to appeal your assessment you must file your appeal, **in writing**, with the BC Assessment Authority by January 31. To do this you must follow the procedure on the reverse of your assessment notice. We will discuss what you should and shouldn't include in your written notice to appeal in the next chapter.

You will then receive a further letter/notification from the BC Assessment Authority with a contact number to schedule an in-person appointment time to present your reasons and supporting evidence to the Property Assessment Review Panel. This is your best opportunity to make your case for a lower assessment. These Review Panel hearings occur between February 1 and March 15. As you can see you don't have much time to prepare your case.

The Property Assessment Review Panel is made up of local citizens just like you and their job is to ensure that the assessments are both fair and equitable. Historically, these Review Panels were trained by the BC Assessment Authority in advance of the hearings. The Provincial Government ended this practice in the early 2000's and they are no longer trained nor influenced in advance by the BC Assessment Authority nor are they predisposed to the valuation the assessor places on any particular property. However, the Review Panel can only adjust an assessment value on the grounds that the assessment was incorrect in some way, based on the notion of not being both "fair and equitable" as we noted in previous chapters.

The Review Panel's decision is then mailed out no later than the end of the first week of April. Generally speaking though, you may get an indication of the Panel's decision at the time of the hearing, just as the gentleman in the introduction did.

If you or the BC Assessment Authority disagrees with the Review Panel's decision, both parties have the right to file a secondary appeal to the Property Assessment Appeal Board on or before April 30. That must be in writing and filed with the requisite administrative fee (currently $30.00 per property at the time of writing). The appeal hearings can occur at any time thereafter. The majority of appeals are resolved at the Review Panel level and most homeowners never go this far.

Preparing For Your Review Panel Hearing
(Or Putting Your Case Together)

This really isn't as hard as it sounds but you will need to put in some leg-work to get the information you need.

Step One: Notice to Appeal

The very first step is to file your Notice to Appeal, as we said in the previous chapter. In the past, the author included his entire written case as to why he believed the assessment was incorrect. He also included a simple written outline of his case, but with no specific details. There are benefits and pitfalls to presenting your case in a structured written format or orally without supporting documentation.

Presenting Your Entire Case with your Notice of Complaint

The first challenge is to collect and organize all your information so that it can be easily compiled and documented and attached to your Notice of Complaint on or before the deadline. Historically, this has given the assessor time to prepare a defense of their assessment valuation.

However, if your case is well prepared and sound, and the assessor is reasonable, it is not unusual for the assessor upon review of the evidence, to agree to a reduced assessment before the actual hearing date. However, we recommend you attend the Review Panel hearing to make sure your case is presented by the BC Assessment Authority as agreed and ensure the values are adjusted. An added benefit is that you can then speak to any matters or questions that may arise from members of the Review Panel, just in case. The overall benefit is that if both parties agree to a reduced assessment, it is rare that the Review Panel will challenge the jointly recommend reduced value.

If you choose to present your entire case in advance, the Review Panel then has an opportunity to more fully understand your issues and concerns. Even if they don't read all of your submission, a well thought out and presented position (and we'll show you how to do that) will stand out from the other appeals by demonstrating your knowledge and support for a change in value which will assist them when deliberating. All of which is in your favor.

Presenting an Outline Only

Forgot everything we said above and you have the benefits and pitfalls of just giving an outline. However, even just an outline should still be well thought out and written with authority – it is unfair to the panel to just say your property assessment is incorrect without further explanation and support. Feel free to state that you have information that indicates the assessment is incorrect, the general basis for the conclusion and give an indication of what you feel the fair value for your property should be. Always close by saying you will present the specifics of your findings at the hearing appointment. And as they said in the old police shows stick to "just the facts".

Step Two: Data Gathering

Fortunately, everything the Assessment Authority does is on the public record so they have made this part of the process very simple.

You can log onto their website at **www.http://evaluebc.bcassessment.ca** (this was previously included in the BC Assessment website, but has since been separated) and download all the assessed values of all your friends and neighbors as well as recent sales information. You can also go to your local assessment authority office and ask to view specific assessment records on microfiche. You will need to know the property's roll number, civic address, or legal description so always have your property assessment notice with you for your reference.

The author created a detailed spreadsheet completed for one of his appeals. This is an invaluable tool in building your case. This spreadsheet can be obtained from the author as a purchaser of this book.

Since the market value was determined using the Direct Comparison Approach and using the basis of "fair and equitable" you can present all the house values in the vicinity of your home if you structure your argument around the quality of the neighborhood and not any specific homes.

How Do You Do That?

You want to see what the average value is for the neighborhood and look to see if your home sticks out like a sore thumb. The concept is that neighborhoods are generally similar in quality. At worse, this gives you a range of values for your area.

We also suggest that you complete an equity review by comparing the increase in assessed values from the previous year to the current year. If, for example, the assessments increased at a rate of 5% year over year but your property received an 8% increase (assuming nothing physically changed to your property) we would note this as part of our case too. Also look at the dollar change year over year. But always remember that a $10 increase on $100 dollars is a 10% increase whereas the same $10 increase on $1000 is just a one percent increase. Not every property in your area will have exactly the same value so consider ranges and trends only.

Once you have reviewed your general neighbourhood assessment values, you have the right to select a total of 8 comparable properties (of your choosing) that the assessor must provide detailed physical information concerning. You will then compare this to your property assessment to determine the price per square foot of physical area.

If you take the area of each house and divide the assessed value by the area this will give you the value per square foot and you can also see if there are any large variances between the properties that way.

So far in your investigation you have three possible areas to base your point: the price of your property against the general neighborhood pricing, an unusual change in assessment for your property compared to others and the value per square foot of your property to others.

And that is only looking at the big picture and not yet looking at direct comparables (or comps for short).

When gathering the neighbors' valuation information make sure you note not only the total valuation but also the value the assessor has placed on the land and the improvements and the size of each and perform the analysis for each component as well as the total.

You can see that using a computerized spreadsheet, such as Excel® or one of the other computerized programs, will save a lot of time doing the math.

Time to introduce another concept or two that will help you really impress the panel.

1. Land generally appreciates (but we will also show you when it doesn't), while improvements depreciate.

As a general rule of economics, land is an asset with scarcity. As the old saying goes "they aren't making anymore". In theory then, outside of a market correction, land should continue to increase in value. On the other hand, unless it is remodeled, improved or even just maintained structures such as buildings, fences, sheds, pools, barns, concrete and landscaping lose value over time.

Tim and I recall one commercial assessment appeal we did for a client who owned a shopping centre in need of substantial repair. We eventually got the value of the shopping center reduced to the land value alone LESS demolition costs of the building. Tim very successfully used the argument that the structure had no value on the market and any buyer would probably have to raze the buildings on the site and start again. That would factor into any price paid for this property as compared to a vacant piece of land that didn't need to have a building removed.

If the building values are going up you may want to make an argument that if major improvements such as a new roof, etc. are needed for your property the cost of those would reduce the market price of your property on the open market. Stated differently, would you pay the same for a house that was identical in every respect to another but the one you wanted to buy required $10,000 (for sake of argument) in repairs? The answer would be no, you would tell the seller that either they can make those repairs and you would pay the price or you would take a $10,000 reduction in order to make those repairs yourself. This is referred to as "deferred maintenance" as we all have friends, neighbours and family that believe their roof will last at least one more year even though a prudent person would replace it and not risk a failed roof and associated water damage.

If the open market pricing is for well-maintained homes requiring little improvement, then the fair and equitable price for a property requiring repairs is less.

However, don't state that the property needs these types of repairs if they don't because the assessor has the right to inspect your property to validate and confirm your concerns as well as verify that their property information is accurate.

Also bear in mind that paint and minor maintenance costs are not generally grounds for a reduced assessment because the principle is that all prudent owners would maintain their homes to an adequate level for the community.

2. Other than adjustments for size, land has a relatively uniform value over a wide geographic area.

If you live in a subdivision chances are that all the lots are about the same size. Performing a square foot calculation as we showed you earlier can highlight any unusual differences.

Another interesting column to include on your spreadsheet is to determine the average value of each component in your neighborhood and then compare each component of each address to the average. This works particularly well with land. For example, if the average assessed land value in your neighborhood is $100,000 (calculated by adding all the land values and then dividing by the number of properties) and your land value is $145,000 then the ratio of your value to the average is 145%. Right now that is just an interesting number.

But if your lot is 10% smaller than the average lot size or even 20% larger than the average lot size then there is something wrong; unless you are located adjacent to a park, golf course or the end of a cul-de-sac, have a view or waterfrontage

As you can see, juggling these numbers - but not lying about them - gives you insight into many areas you could point out to the panel where they could find a reason to lower your assessed value.

Remember that the panel needs information to justify their reasons for an adjustment. The more reasons you can give them, the easier it is for them to make a decision in your favor.

Step three: Direct Comparison

Are you friends with a real estate agent? Want to become a real estate agent's friend?

The simplest way to get comps on comparable houses is to speak with someone in the business and ask for historic **sales** to July 1 of comparable houses (year built, size, number of bedrooms, amenities, etc.) in a fairly tight radius of your home. Get pictures, listing information if their office helped sell or buy those homes, etc.

Then compare your home to those. Remember though do not look at the listing prices but rather the price the houses sold for on or around July 1. Ideally get five comps.

Here is what to look for in these comps:

Look for sales of homes in neighborhoods in the vicinity of yours that are of a similar quality to your neighborhood. The important criteria are that the neighborhoods must not be across town or in another city and the neighborhoods must be of a similar quality. The assessor will know if you are using an inferior neighborhood and attempting to do a direct comparison without making an adjustment for quality.

Look for sales of similar style of houses, townhouses or condos to yours, if possible. While not as important as other factors, showing the Appeal Board pictures of houses that look like your house gives them a sense that the houses you used are comparable to yours. For example showing a picture of a one storey mid-century bungalow to another one storey mid-century bungalow leaves a stronger impression than contrasting it to a two storey farmhouse even if the two properties are similar in every other respect.

The comparable houses, townhouses or condos should ideally have the same or similar features, inside and out, such as those as noted below:
- Number of parking spaces
- Garage or carport

- Yard amenities such as play area, outdoor kitchen, pool, spa, mature landscaping, deck, porch, out buildings, fencing, etc.
- Exterior finish (stucco, brick, stone, wood)
- Number of rooms (all rooms)
- Number of bedrooms
- Number of bathrooms and half baths and the finish in each
- Ensuite
- Fireplace(s)
- Formal living room
- Formal dining room
- Family room
- Kitchen finish (white or stainless steel appliances for example)
- Age and style of interior decorating
- A finished or unfinished basement
- Interior finishes

The other houses should be in the same size range as yours and the lot size should be the same size.

The lot should have the same features such as connection to city or community water and waste, have the same types of views (water, mountain, city or none of these), be situated the same – such as on a corner, if your lot is on a corner.

Do not include any homes that have attached businesses as these become too complicated to adjust for like value. Examples of this would be homes with an auto repair facility in a large building on the lot, homes with corner grocery stores attached, etc.

Likewise, don't attempt to fool the appeal board with comparables of properties inferior to yours. Showing the price paid for a 'handyman special' as a comparison to your well-maintained house will not work.

There is another type of residential property that you should not use in your list of comparables. If you live on the edge of town or in a semi-rural area you may find that some of your neighbours have acreages that qualify for lower assessments with farm classification status. This is a different class of residential property that creates an artificially lower assessed value.

Making Adjustments

Once you have found a few good comparable properties and obtained good pictures of both the neighborhoods and the comparable properties, you will need to make adjustments for differences between each of those and your property. Naturally, if you have followed the suggestions on selecting comparables there won't need to be many adjustments. But bear in mind that no two properties are identical and some adjustments are likely.

An adjustment is either adding to or subtracting from the comparable's value (the price it sold for or is assessed at) to adjust it to your house. Never adjust your value in this part of the exercise as it gets too confusing to present if some comparable house features result in value changes and your property's value also changes too.

When we have discussed this with others they wonder why we don't suggest adjusting the subject property to the comparables if our goal is to lower the assessment? The problem lies in setting a consistent benchmark. Cast your memory back to high school or university science experiments. You'll recall that when comparing several things it was always helpful to have a 'control' or an unchanging thing to compare to. The same principle applies. It is always easier and less confusing to adjust several comparables to one static and known property than it is to compare one to several different properties. The other reason to use your property as the 'control' or "base" is that you are intimately familiar with every aspect of your property. You may not know the other comparable properties as well.

Here is how to make your adjustments. Remember, items that make your property more valuable than the comparables mean that you ADD value to the comparable property. Items that make the comparable property more valuable than yours will mean you will have to SUBTRACT value from their selling price.

Each plus and minus item needs to be listed with a value attached. You will then have a net difference.

For example, let's say your property has an ocean view but doesn't have a garage and has an assessed value of $525,000 (your property will always be referred to as the "subject property") and comparable property A is very similar to yours except that it doesn't have an ocean view but does have a garage. It sold for $375,000.

You would ADD to comparable property A an amount for the ocean view and SUBTRACT for the garage. Lets assume, that your research showed that home with an ocean view averaged $100,000 more than homes without one. Likewise, a garage added $50,000 to the selling price of a home as compared to one without one. Here is what it would look like:

Items	Subject Property (your property)	Comparable A
Assessed value or selling price	$525,000	$375,000
Ocean View (add)		+$100,000
Garage (subtract)		- $ 50,000
Adjusted Value	$525,000	$425,000

What this fictitious example would indicate is that, after adjusting for differences in conditions, comparable property A should have sold for about $425,000 if it were reasonably identical to your property. Therefore, you would argue that your property should be assessed at $425,000 and not $525,000 based on a comparable sale.

Looking at this example, you may be tempted to argue that your property is actually valued at the same as comparable A (at $375,000); however, by not acknowledging and showing reasonable adjustment results in doubt in the panel member's minds. Your job is not only to provide the data, but to convince the panel that you know what you are doing. This gives you an air of confidence as well as making their job easier. For the same reason, Tim starts each one of his appeal presentations with a list of his credentials and work experience.

Keep in mind that you will have several of these comparables and they won't all point to the same adjusted value. You will have a range of value.

There is one other adjustment that needs to be made unless, and in the unlikely event, all your comparables sold on July 1. You will need to "time adjust" the selling price of the comparable sales by the month over month change in the average price to or from the July 1st date. This information is easily available from your local real estate board or from the real estate agent who has been helping you gather this information. This time adjustment can be positive or negative depending on what the residential real estate market was doing before and after July 1st. The market changes in terms of demand for homes and that may be different than townhouses and condos in your neighbourhood.

How to Find Value Adjustment Figures

The first way is to ask your friendly real estate agent that has been helping you so far. They have a fairly good sense of value adjustments because they are in the market daily.

The second way is to ask the professional assessors at the BC Assessment Authority. While this may seem like an unlikely source this is the safest information to use. Here is how to get it.

Earlier you read that you can ask the assessor for eight comparables of your choosing and obtain detailed information on these. We have found that the detail provides the items for adjustment (but they may have missed some things because the assessors can't visit every property every year and this is part of your leverage) and when you politely question them about the differences and the values they use, they will freely give you that information. However, it is important not to interrogate the assessor. At this point they are your ally and they have the information you want.

Obviously, if you also have a real estate agent as a friend you can compare what the two say the adjustment should be.

Some adjustments are not as subjective as, say, the value of an ocean view, verses ocean glimpses or comparing an ocean view to a water (lake or river) view or to a city view. Those are highly subjective adjustments as compared to a quantifiable adjustment such as for size, which can be easily measured. The same goes for a quiet cul-de-sac location versus a busy traffic corner or close proximity to commercial/industrial uses.

Once you have determined the average price per square foot for both the assessed value and for the selling prices it is a simple matter to multiply that rate ($/sf) by the differences in the house or lot size. However, just as the price of a large box of cereal is not directly proportionally more expensive than the smaller box, so too is real estate. That makes sense since some costs of construction remain the same irrespective of the size of the building and land is always less expensive per unit the more one has.

Therefore, when looking at the average price per square foot, pick a range of sizes as close as possible to what you have.

Preparing the Argument for the Property Assessment Review Panel

We think this is the easy and fun part. This is the part where you look at all the data and information you have like a detective or a trial lawyer you see on TV, and see if you can craft a convincing story to make your point. This is where you look for anomalies in the data or patterns that support your case. IT IS CRITICAL THAT YOUR PRESENTATION BE CONDENSED TO 15 MINUTES OR LESS TO MAKE YOUR POINTS.

We believe in our "Rule of Three" in creating and presenting your case for a lower assessment. Our Rule of Three is simply to find and state three reasons why the stated original assessment should be changed. If you can't find three, that's OK, one or two will work. Our 'rule' helps us do a few things:

1. If we are looking at the data and have only found one or two basis for our case arguments we will keep looking a bit more to see if there is a third. Sometimes just by combining our previous two findings we come up with the third argument. Having more than one reason for the review panel to grant your reduction goes a long way in helping them help you.

2. It focuses our presentation. Rather than coming up with an overabundance of data and information to throw at the panel members, hoping that they can then discern the information and come up with a reason for a reduction themselves, we focus our attention on no more than three really good arguments with lots of data to back up each.

3. Any more than three reasons will become distracting to the panel members. You want to simply and clearly provide them with a few reasons why you believe a reduction is warranted.

4. It keeps the presentation short. Too many times we have seen unprepared homeowners ramble on during their presentation to the review panel. This can end up being a frustrating process for everyone. Giving the panel three distinct, focused and clear reasons shows them you have done your research and are acting professionally – as a result, they are more likely to reward your efforts.

5. If the assessor can convince the review panel that one of your arguments is not valid, you have two back-ups. However, we don't suggest that you roll out only one at a time, wait for the response and if is not favorable, try another reason, and if that one doesn't

work, try the third. The review panel may quickly lose patience and you may never get to your second and third reasons. Instead, you should state all three arguments in your presentation. This just gives the assessor more to have to counter in their arguments. If the assessor can only shoot down one of the three, then by all means agree that was your weakest argument, but point out the other two remain very valid because the assessor only found an issue with one.

The Review Panel Hearing

Before we discuss the actual hearing, we must emphasis, that unless you previously ask for an adjournment or postponement of your review panel hearing, you must be on-time for the hearing! **<u>NO EXCEPTIONS</u>**. The panel will take a no show as agreement to the assessed value and will not permit a subsequent hearing. Plan accordingly when you receive your notice of the Review Panel Hearing.

Your written presentation should be the same as the verbal presentation. You may not always comfortable with public speaking, even in front of just two or three strangers. As a result, you may prefer to read the written presentation at the meeting and that is why we have outlined both the written submission and the presentation as one.

Prior to going to the Review Panel meeting print at least five copies of your written presentation. This way you can give one copy to each panel member, one copy to the assessor, who will also attend the meeting, and one copy for you to read from.

Formatting the presentation

Even if you have never given a presentation before you can give a short, simple presentation to the review panel using the formula we give you.

There are a few things to keep in mind as you write your presentation.

Make Friends with the Panel

Recognize that the review panel is neutral. You want to win them over, so the tone of both the written and verbal presentations must be polite. It is common for frustration to sound angry or even turn into anger. If you flip back to the introduction you'll see that the gentleman in that case quickly became angry and defensive. He then alienated the panel members by telling them they didn't live in his area, inferring that they didn't know what they were doing. In short, he didn't win any friends on the panel.

Give the Facts and Data

Remember too that your presentation must stick only to the facts and data concerning what you believe to be the value of your property on July 1. There should be no discussion about how poor the garbage collection is, how few police officers there are, etc. The review panel can do nothing about those things. The panel may feel that the appellant (that's you) is unprepared and does not have a justification for the requested reduction.

Know the Rules We Set Out Earlier

Keep in mind that the assessor must abide by certain professional codes of conduct when setting and defending an assessed value. You don't have those restrictions. Now this may sound like you can lie or present misinformation or be unethical in your presentation. We don't advocate any of those. In fact, just the opposite. You must always be honest, present full information to support your position and be completely ethical. What we mean is that you should phrase your arguments and reasons in terms that show the assessor didn't follow the rules they are suppose to follow. More on that later.

Start with a brief introduction.

Here is an example:

"Good day ladies and gentlemen (as appropriate). My name is _____. My property at [address] has been assessed at $XXX,000. Today I will present three reasons why this property value should be $123,456; using the accepted principles that the assessment value must be fair and equitable."

Work from the Big Picture to Your Property

Structure your presentation starting with the bigger picture of the values of homes in your area, then your specific neighborhood or block (if applicable) and then to your specific property.

Here are some of the questions you want to answer in support of your presentation.

The Area

Does your area have the same social and economic statistics? You don't need to be a statistician to know this. Just driving around and talking with your neighbors will guide you. And you still can ask your friendly real estate agent for this information too. However, if your area is generally the same and all your comps come from within that area tell the panel that. Don't assume they know your area.

That way, if the assessor presents a comparable in support of their valuation from outside the area, you can state that the neighborhoods are not the same. This plants a seed of doubt in the minds of the panel members. Be aware however, they may ask you why you feel they are not the same.

The Immediate Neighborhood

Next, look at the assessed values in your neighborhood. If your property assessment is notably higher than the others, tell the panel this too. While you are comparing apples and oranges in this case (since each house is different), you have set the stage when you said your area is comparably the same.

Land Values

Then look at the per square foot value of the land in your immediate area. Is the assessed value of your land significantly more than other property in your area? Show this to the panel. If you know how to create charts in a software program such as Microsoft's Excel®, please create a chart showing the difference. When you outline this portion of your presentation give the panel reasons why your property should be the same or even less than your neighbor's land value.

Less? Yes. Although land values share more in common with every other parcel than a building does with every other building, there are still variables. For example, you may find in your data that all the land in your area is in a very narrow per square foot value range. This may occur when the computer program calculated land values. Does this mean you should attempt to get a lower land value on your assessment? After all, you may reason, it is the same as everyone else. However, should *all the land* be the same per square foot value? Land that has views; is against green-space such as a park or ravine; is next to a playground or school; or is at the end of a cul-d-sac or dead end street is more valuable than land that is not and a lot more valuable than land under high power lines, backing onto a freeway, or an industrial plant, etc.

If all the land values are similar, pick out those lots that are better positioned than yours and tell the board why those lots are better and suggest a reduction in your per square foot value that is comfortable to you based on your research.

And contrary to the popular belief that land always appreciates in value, it can depreciate. For example, one of the author's relatives purchased a home that had distant water views. Those views made up part of the purchase price of the home. The year after purchasing the home, the assessor valued the home at what they paid for it. They never appealed their assessment so every year thereafter their assessment grew. Unfortunately, so did the trees between their property and those water views. By showing the review panel the difference in the views from pictures they had taken when they bought the home and at the time of the review they were able to argue that the current inflated land value was still based on the views they no longer enjoyed. Have conditions changed in your area that affects the value of your property?

Other negative issues can be the discovery of an old underground oil tank that must be removed or that has failed and requires cleanup. Land erosion due to creek or river course changes. Zoning changes in the neighbourhood that increase commercial or industrial activities and traffic.

Computer Generated Math

The software the Assessment Authority uses is very complex, that, frankly we don't understand. Fortunately, none of us need to understand it to make it work in our favor from time to time. Ultimately, the output of the program comes down to a mathematical formula that is statistically correct. Remember there is always a margin of error in statistics. Here is how you can use that to your advantage.

Let's say that from your data gathering you have determined that the range in total assessed value increases from the present year to the previous year is between 5 and 7% and the average increase is 5.5%. Is your increase higher than the average or the range? If you have made no changes to your property that would account for the above normal increase ask for a reduction pointing out that the increase was due to a computer generated outcome and not from a change in conditions. The computer outcome in this case was flawed. Yes, blame the computer!

Is your home larger than most or already one of the higher priced homes in the area? If the percentage increase on your property is within the same range as all the other houses point out that these types of houses don't increase at the same percentage rate as other houses, noting too that a 10% increase on $1000.00 is ten times more than the same 10% increase on $100.00. "Obviously, the program made a mistake by applying the same percentage to the overall average value in the area", is a comment you may wish to make.

The Home

Now is the time to show the differences in each of the comparables to your home. The chart you completed is all that is needed here with a paragraph or two about the research you did, specifically noting that except where there are differences and adjustments made, you feel these comparables fairly represent the values at July 1 and cite the sources for your adjusting data. For example, you may state something along the lines of:

"The adjustments were made with values I received from the Assessor's own office and from a local real estate agent who has specialized in residential sales in my area for over 15 years, and who has sold 243 homes in the past three years."

Don't forget to present the pictures of each comparable property and pictures of your own property. As they say, a picture is worth a thousand words and Review Panels are famous for asking for picture evidence.

The Adjusted Value

The last part of your presentation should always be a reminder of your requested adjusted value.

Keep in mind that the Review Panel may choose to give you all, some or none of your requested decrease. In some cases, they may actually, increase your assessment. Our experience is the chair of the panel may give you an indication of what their decision will be at the time of the review hearing, and then ask if we agree with their decision.

Obviously, if you got the reduction you asked for you should be pleased and tell them you agree with it.

If the panel awards something less than your requested amount you have two options: accept their adjustment or negotiate.

When You Want to Negotiate

We suggest that if the panel agrees to more than half of your requested reduction you seriously consider accepting their decision. Naturally, if we are talking a very large reduction and the difference between their proposed adjustment and your request is large you should reserve your position and seek further advice. Ideally, in those cases you should use a professional from the start since the stakes are so high.

If their offer is less than half your well researched and documented reduction ask the panel to explain how they came to the decision and what points in your presentation you could clarify for them so they 'can get closer to your request'.

By using the phrase 'can get closer to your request'; you are signaling a mutual opportunity to look at different numbers.

If they say there is nothing you could add, you can polite say this:

"I'm, afraid I don't understand how you arrived at that proposed number or where the data or logic went wrong. Because, if my data is correct, the requested adjustment is supported by the data – which is the basis of the definition of fair and equitable market value upon which my property **must be** assessed by the Assessment Authority."

You'll note that this is the time when the earlier chapters in understanding the process come into play. This phrase subtly suggests you might bring this to the next level of appeal.

Then *before they have time to respond* add that:

"I understand there is a lot of information presented and a lot of other property owners you have to hear, so to make it easier for everyone would we all agree to….." then propose a new assessed value being in a range of the greater of half way between their adjustment and your request and a little more than half of your requested adjustment.

Then finish your comments with a conciliatory phrase such as:

"At this value, I feel my property is in the range of fair market value and can be supported by the assessor and the panel by the information I've presented today. I would also like to thank you for your assistance today."

The Review Panel may come back with another number, may reiterate their previous position or accept your revised value. They will also want the assessor to concur with their adjusted value too since either the assessment authority or the property owner can appeal the Review Panel's decision to the next level.

Your research and professionalism may weigh on the assessor's mind as they consider whether or not they should accept the panel's decision. They may wonder if they want to tangle with you again at the next level of appeal.

Even if you do get any immediate feedback and a proposed decision from the panel remember that it is not complete until it is a recorded written decision; so retain all your records. You will receive their decision in the mail after the review panel as recorded their decision.

If you still disagree you can take your appeal to the next step and repeat the process. If you did present all your case before the Review Panel meeting, please note that the assessor will now have all your arguments and time to prepare counter arguments to support their valuation.

If the panel's written decision says you got what you asked for in a reduced value,

CONGRATULATIONS!

You have not only saved yourself money this year but in the years following.

But you are not quite finished yet. Keep the decision with the revised value and compare that to the value stated on your tax bill notice. The values should match. If they don't match immediately contact both the Assessment Authority and the taxation office that issued you the tax bill and show them the written decision.

The Final Step

This is the last step in the process, or the first step if you are reading this BEFORE your receive your assessment notice.

Call your local assessor.

If you went through each step in this guide and ended at the Review Panel you will know them on sight. The staff at the Assessment Authority rarely hear from you, their customers. They will appreciate the call.

If you got the reduction you requested from the Review Panel, call and thank the assessor for their professionalism and assistance through the process.

If you didn't get all of the adjustment you wanted or you have read this guide but haven't yet received your current assessment notice you want to set an appointment with the assessor BEFORE they finalize their next roll. Here is why.

The assessor will work with you to determine a fair market value if you follow this guide and present your arguments well. Until the assessor signs off on the roll they have not placed their professional reputations on the line with your property assessment. Once they have completed the roll they are in the position of defending their opinion of value as well as their position and professional reputation. Until then they are more likely to work with you to arrive at a value that is correct and so that they will not be challenged by you in the future.

If you didn't get the full adjustment you feel the data shows and you believe there is still room to reduce your assessment on the next year's assessment, you will have a better chance of obtaining your goal by working with the assessor before hand rather than in the challenging and somewhat confrontational theatre of the Review Panel. Remember too that some of the Review Panel members may be on next year's panel. If the Panel sees you showing up time and again for the same property they may not grant you a full hearing on the basis that they previously rendered an opinion, if the market evidence and issues haven't changed.

If you are reading this guide before your assessment notice, now is the time to work with your assessor to reduce your upcoming assessment. You will still need to go through all the steps we outline as though you were about to submit your evidence to the Review Panel. Rather than presenting this to the Panel however, you are going to use it "to help the assessor correct data problems in their system". You want to time this so you do your fact finding and prepare your position as soon after July 1 as possible. First, complete your entire presentation then arrange a meeting to review your information with the Assessment Authority and discuss an acceptable valuation.

Ideally, this discussion should be completed before the September long weekend. This is because the Assessment Roll starts to be compiled in September and October and your preferred position is to influence the value in advance rather than correct it afterwards.

For The Mathematically Inclined

By now you have determined that lowering your assessed value will lower your tax burden as compared to the original value since the taxation rate, or mill rate, is applied to each $1000.00 in value.

However, there are two other benefits to this exercise.

If you are successful in lowering your assessed value, the computer software at the BC Assessment Authority will use that lower assessment value for their future value adjustments. As a result the savings will continue year after year as compared to not challenging your property assessment.

The third benefit, in addition to an immediate theoretical saving against what you would have had to pay in taxes and the long term benefit of that year over year, is the possibility of a real reduction in your personal real estate taxes compared to the previous year. How is this possible?

Remember that we want the denominator of all the values to be really big? If the increase in your value is less than the average value and if the mill rate is held in check, then it is mathematically possible that you will see a real reduction in the property taxes on your property.

Here is a simplified version of the math.

Lets assume that the municipal budget increases 3% and the total assessed value upon which the mill rate is calculated also increases 3% across all 9 rate categories, then the two will have increased the same and will cancel each other out and there would be no increase in the actual tax bill.

Using the example above, and having achieved just a 2% increase in your assessed value, your property will be below the average and you should see a net reduction in taxes as compared to the previous year.

Conclusion

We trust we have accomplished the following:

- Convinced you that it is your right and responsibility to seek the most correct value for your property;
- Provided a method to obtain and analyze the vast amount of data that is freely available to you; and
- Prepare and present a compelling case to the Appeal Board, or ideally to the assessor before the assessment roll is ever created.

Please remember though, that it will be the judgment of the panel members that determines the success of your appeal for a lower assessment. They are there to assist you in obtaining a fair and equitable value.

Using the process outlined in this book, we have successfully reduced our own residential assessed value and pocketed the savings. We want you to have the same success.

For more information:

To obtain the FREE spreadsheet referenced in this book, email **AppealBC@attainmentpress.com** and note "Spreadsheet" in the subject line.

To Contact Tim Down about his residential or commercial property assessment appeal practice email:

Tim Down, AACI, P. App, CAE, RI
PacWest Commercial Real Estate Advisors
E-mail: info@pacwestrealestate.ca

To contact Peter Morris regarding his commercial real estate consulting practice:

Peter D. Morris CRX, SCLS, SCSM, SCMD
Greenstead Consulting Group
E-mail: pdmorris@greensteadcg.com

22141665R00038

Made in the USA
San Bernardino, CA
09 January 2019